THE PRESIDENT

THE PRESIDENT

by Keith Brandt
Illustrated by Bob Dole

Library of Congress Cataloging-in-Publication Data

Brandt, Keith, (date)
    President.

    Summary: Explains the powers and duties of the presi-
dent of the United States, and the procedure by which a
new one is chosen every four years.
    1. Presidents—United States—Juvenile literature.
[1. Presidents.   2. United States—Politics and govern-
ment]   I. Dole, Bob, ill.   II. Title.
JK517.B73   1985   353.03'1   84-2652
ISBN 0-8167-0268-3 (lib. bdg.)
ISBN 0-8167-0269-1 (pbk.)

This edition published in 2002.

Printed in the United States of America.

10 9 8 7 6 5 4 3 2

Every four years the people of the United States of America elect a President. This practice, set down in the U.S. Constitution, began with the election of George Washington in 1789. It has continued this way ever since.

On the first Tuesday after the first Monday in November, every fourth year, the presidential election takes place. The person who is elected then takes the oath of office and becomes President on the following January 20. The two and a half months between the election and the inauguration make it possible for there to be an orderly changeover from one administration to another.

The people of the United States have been electing Presidents in this manner for so long that it seems to us to be a normal, sensible way of doing it. But it was very unusual when George Washington became President. That is because he was the first person in the history of the world to be elected as a national leader according to a written constitution. Until then, countries were ruled by monarchs who inherited a throne or by tyrants who seized power by force.

Although the people of the United States elect the President, they do so indirectly. Actually the voters in each state elect a certain number of men and women known as "electors." And it is these electors who vote, state by state, for the President.

The number of electors for each state equals the number of senators and representatives that state sends to the U.S. Congress. For example, California, which has a large population, has fifty-five electors. Wyoming, which has a small population, has only three electors.

The electors of each state, along with three from the District of Columbia, cast all their votes for the candidate who gets the most votes in their state. This means that, if candidate A gets just one vote more than any other candidate, all of that state's electoral votes go to candidate A.

There are more than five hundred presidential electors—and each one has just one job to do. The electors meet in a body called the Electoral College, and they cast their votes, state by state. When they are done, the winning candidate officially becomes the President-elect. Then, on Inauguration Day, the President-elect takes the oath of office from the Chief Justice of the United States Supreme Court and becomes the nation's President.

The Constitution says who may be a candidate for the office of President. The President must be a natural-born citizen. This rule also applies to the Vice President, who takes office as President if the President dies or resigns or is removed from office.

The President must also be at least thirty-five years old at the time of inauguration, and must have lived at least fourteen years in the United States.

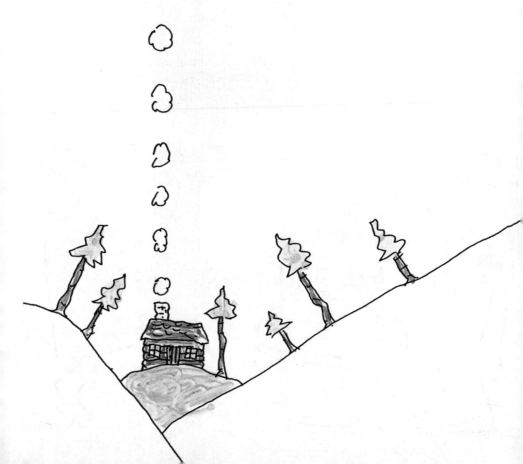

The Constitution describes the President's job. The President is commander in chief of the armed forces and has the power to grant pardons and reprieves for offenses against the United States.

With the advice and consent of the Senate, the President makes treaties with foreign nations and appoints ambassadors and judges of the U.S. Supreme Court and other federal courts. The President also appoints the heads of many departments, which are part of the executive—or presidential—branch of government. These department heads are members of the President's cabinet.

The U.S. Constitution makes no mention of a presidential cabinet. But when Congress met in 1789, it established three executive departments. They were the Department of State, the Department of the Treasury, and the Department of War. Each of these departments was to be headed by a secretary appointed by the President. And the secretaries of these departments made up the first presidential cabinet.

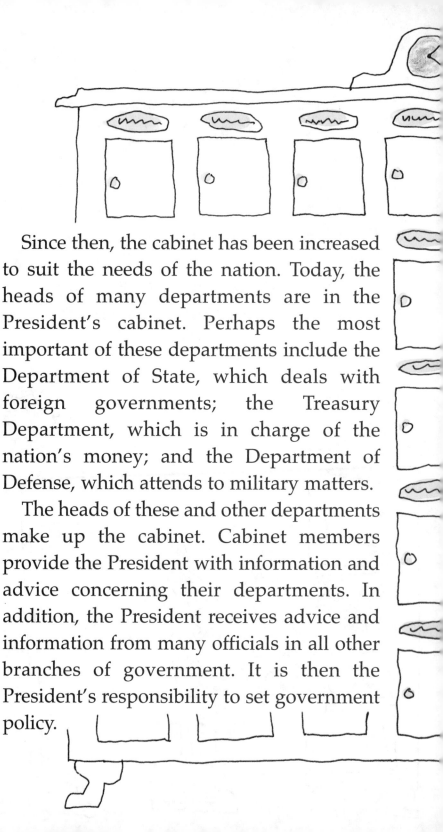

Since then, the cabinet has been increased to suit the needs of the nation. Today, the heads of many departments are in the President's cabinet. Perhaps the most important of these departments include the Department of State, which deals with foreign governments; the Treasury Department, which is in charge of the nation's money; and the Department of Defense, which attends to military matters.

The heads of these and other departments make up the cabinet. Cabinet members provide the President with information and advice concerning their departments. In addition, the President receives advice and information from many officials in all other branches of government. It is then the President's responsibility to set government policy.

Much of the President's time is devoted to meetings. Each day, advisors bring the President up to date on important events in the nation and the world. These briefings help the President make decisions on a wide variety of subjects.

As America's chief executive, the President also meets with the leaders of foreign countries. These meetings let the President take a major role in international affairs. For example, by meeting with representatives of feuding countries, the President may offer them an opportunity for resolving their differences and reaching a peaceful solution to their problems.

While these serious matters are among the most significant parts of the presidency, the President also has a ceremonial role. The President welcomes kings and queens and other noted foreign visitors to the country, and greets a broad range of other visitors at the White House, in Washington, D.C.

The White House is the official home of

the President, and every day many people come to see this historic mansion. Some of these visitors take a tour of the public sections of the White House. Others are lucky enough to meet with the President in the Oval Office, outside in the Rose Garden, or at a luncheon or dinner served in one of the dining rooms.

On any given day, the President may chat with religious and civic groups, Boy Scouts, Girl Scouts, scholars and scientists, and citizens from throughout the nation. For these people, it is an honor they will never forget. For the President, it is a way of keeping in touch with the American public.

The President is not always at the White House. There are international conferences to attend, foreign countries to visit, and speeches to be made all over the United States.

In addition, every President needs some time to rest from the heavy demands of the job. For this, each President chooses some place away from Washington as a summer, or vacation, White House. The government also provides a presidential retreat, called Camp David, in the hills of Maryland.

But the President can never be alone for very long. Secret Service agents constantly protect the President and the presidential family. Because Presidents have been assassinated and others attacked by would-be assassins, it would not be safe to let the President go unguarded at any time.

That is why the President travels in bullet-proof cars, on special trains, and aboard the presidential plane, called *Air Force One.* The Secret Service also tries to keep presidential travel routes secret and check out the people who will be near the President.

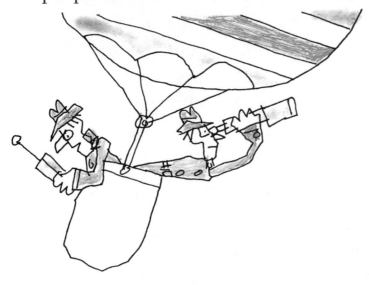

As the U.S. has grown in size and importance, so have the powers of the President. Through the cabinet departments, and many other federal agencies, the President has influence over government spending, economic and social policies, and decisions that affect the nation at home and abroad.

The President of the United States is one of the most powerful people in the world. Still, there are definite limits to presidential powers. And Presidents who have tried to go beyond these limits have been stopped by Congress or by the Supreme Court.

The Supreme Court can prevent a President from using powers not granted in the Constitution. If the President does not listen to the Supreme Court, the U.S. Congress can impeach and try the President. This means that the President is first impeached, or accused, by the members of the House of Representatives. Then the President is put on trial in the Senate. If guilty, the President is then removed from office.

In the history of the United States, there have been some great Presidents and a few bad Presidents. But most have worked hard to do what has been called the toughest job in the entire world—that of the President of the United States of America.